My

365 Day

Guided Journal.

*

Tony T Robinson.

ISBN:1522717595
ISBN-13:978-1522717591

*

© 2015 Tony T Robinson.

All rights reserved.

ISBN-13:978-1522717591

DEDICATION

*

This book is dedicated to everyone who is committed to self-exploration through journaling and who believes in the power and purpose of self-development.

*

Other Books by Tony T Robinson.

*

101 Journal Questions for Women.

*

101 Self-Discovery Journal Prompts.

*

101 Quick and Easy Confidence Quotes.

*

101 Confidence Quotes that will change your life.

*

101 I AM Power Affirmations.

*

THIS JOURNAL BELONGS TO

____

ADD A PHOTO
OF YOURSELF
HERE.

ABOUT THIS JOURNAL.

*

There are many Journals available ranging from ones with blank pages through to guided journals. In my first journal 101 Self Discovery Journal prompts I used single trigger words to allow the user to free associate, explore and delve into their unconscious.

In my last journal 101 Journal Questions for Women I opted for the more direct approach incorporating a variety of questions requiring the writer to “dig deep” as well as questions designed to boost their self-esteem and confidence.

In this journal I have used a combination of both open and direct questions which provides an area of focus as well as having the freedom to explore your thoughts and ideas.

This is a 365 day journal with daily headings from Monday to Sunday. I have purposely not included dates so that you can start your journal from the beginning of the book at any time of the year but please feel free to add the date if you want to.

There are many guided journals including prayer and gratitude journals. I have chosen to incorporate these and other ideas such as setting weekly goals, law of attraction, writing down affirmations and quotes that you like as well as a space for you to record your daily thoughts and a weekly review every Sunday.

Although this is not an art journal there is no reason why you cannot be creative and use different coloured pens and different writing styles, feel free to add doodles and use colouring pencils to decorate the pages either by highlighting text or as a colourful background. *(I would not recommend using felt tips pens or markers as they may bleed through the page)*

I have also included a few lists where you can keep a record of things that you have done throughout the year as well as things about yourself. I think this is particularly fun especially when you have completed several journals because then you can look back and compare them and see how you and your life has changed over the years.

So on that note I will let you begin your first entry and I hope you have a great year.

Much love Tony T.

List your Achievements/accomplishments.

Keep a list of every film you see at the Movies.

Make a list of every Book you read.

Keep a list of your Favorite things.

These things make me Happy.

Days/Nights out and Special Occasions.

MONDAY.

My Goal for this week is –

____

____

____

Today I am Grateful for –

____

____

____

Daily thought.

____

____

____

____

____

____

____

____

____

____

____

TUESDAY.

I am Thankful for -

Today I Pray for -

Daily thought.

WEDNESDAY.

I am Grateful for -

Today I feel -

Daily thought.

THURSDAY.

I am Thankful for -

Today I would like to Attract -

Daily thought.

FRIDAY.

Today I am Grateful for -

I Wish -

Daily thought.

SATURDAY.

I am Thankful for -

Write or copy a Positive Affirmation -

Daily thought.

SUNDAY REVIEW.

What has been the best and worst part of your week?

____

____

____

____

____

____

____

____

____

____

Self-Refection / Self–Awareness.

____

____

____

____

____

____

____

____

____

____

MONDAY.

My Goal for this week is -

I am Thankful for -

Thought of the Day.

TUESDAY.

I am Grateful for -

I need -

Thought of the Day.

WEDNESDAY.

I am Thankful for -

Write down a quote that you like.

Daily thought.

THURSDAY.

I am Grateful for -

I Believe -

Random thought.

FRIDAY.

I am Thankful for -

____

____

____

Today I Pray for -

____

____

____

____

I Promise -

____

____

____

____

Pay yourself a compliment.

____

____

____

____

____

SATURDAY.

I am Grateful for -

I Can-

Daily thought.

SUNDAY REVIEW.

What has been the best and worst part of your week?

Self-Refection / Self–Awareness.

MONDAY.

My Goal for this week is -

I am Thankful for -

Thought of the Day.

TUESDAY.

I am Grateful for -

I Know -

Daily thought.

WEDNESDAY.

I am Thankful for -

____

____

____

I Attract -

____

____

____

____

____

I Will -

____

____

____

____

Write or copy a Positive Affirmation.

____

____

____

____

THURSDAY.

I am Grateful for -

Today I Pray for -

Thought of the Day.

FRIDAY.

I am Thankful for -

I AM -

Daily thought.

SATURDAY.

I am Grateful for -

___

___

___

I Promise -

___

___

___

___

___

Daily thought.

___

___

___

___

___

___

___

___

___

___

SUNDAY REVIEW.

What has been the best and worst part of your week?

Self-Refection / Self–Awareness.

MONDAY.

My Goal for this week is -

I am Thankful for -

Thought of the Day.

TUESDAY.

I am Thankful for -

I Love -

Thought of the Day.

WEDNESDAY.

I am Grateful for -

I Feel -

Today I Pray for -

Today I Attract -

THURSDAY.

I am Thankful for -

Today I let go of -

Thought of the Day.

FRIDAY.

I am Grateful for -

I Promise -

Write or copy a Positive Affirmation.

I love my Life because -

SATURDAY.

I am Thankful for -

I Forgive -

Daily Thought.

SUNDAY REVIEW.

What has been the best and worst part of your week?

Self-Refection / Self–Awareness.

MONDAY.

My Goal for this week is –

Today I am Grateful for –

Daily thought.

TUESDAY.

I am Thankful for -

Today I Pray for -

Daily thought.

WEDNESDAY.

I am Grateful for -

Today I feel -

Daily thought.

THURSDAY.

I am Thankful for -

Today I would like to Attract -

Daily thought.

FRIDAY.

Today I am Grateful for -

I Wish -

Daily thought.

SATURDAY.

I am Thankful for -

Write or copy a Positive Affirmation -

Daily thought.

SUNDAY REVIEW.

What has been the best and worst part of your week?

Self-Refection / Self–Awareness.

MONDAY.

My Goal for this week is -

I am Thankful for -

Thought of the Day.

TUESDAY.

I am Grateful for -

I need -

Thought of the Day.

WEDNESDAY.

I am Thankful for -

Write down a quote that you like.

Daily thought.

THURSDAY.

I am Grateful for -

____

____

____

I Believe -

____

____

____

____

____

____

Random thought.

____

____

____

____

____

____

____

____

____

FRIDAY.

I am Thankful for -

Today I Pray for -

I Promise -

Pay yourself a compliment.

SATURDAY.

I am Grateful for -

I Can-

Daily thought.

SUNDAY REVIEW.

What has been the best and worst part of your week?

Self-Refection / Self–Awareness.

MONDAY.

My Goal for this week is -

I am Thankful for -

Thought of the Day.

TUESDAY.

I am Grateful for -

I Know -

Daily thought.

WEDNESDAY.

I am Thankful for -

I Attract -

I Will -

Write or copy a Positive Affirmation.

THURSDAY.

I am Grateful for -

Today I Pray for -

Thought of the Day.

FRIDAY.

I am Thankful for -

I AM -

Daily thought.

SATURDAY.

I am Grateful for -

I Promise -

Daily thought.

SUNDAY REVIEW.

What has been the best and worst part of your week?

Self-Refection / Self–Awareness.

MONDAY.

My Goal for this week is -

I am Thankful for -

Thought of the Day.

TUESDAY.

I am Thankful for -

I Love -

Thought of the Day.

WEDNESDAY.

I am Grateful for -

I Feel -

Today I Pray for -

Today I Attract -

THURSDAY.

I am Thankful for -

Today I let go of -

Thought of the Day.

FRIDAY.

I am Grateful for -

I Promise -

Write or copy a Positive Affirmation.

I love my Life because -

SATURDAY.

I am Thankful for -

I Forgive -

Daily Thought.

SUNDAY REVIEW.

What has been the best and worst part of your week?

Self-Refection / Self–Awareness.

MONDAY.

My Goal for this week is –

Today I am Grateful for –

Daily thought.

TUESDAY.

I am Thankful for -

Today I Pray for -

Daily thought.

WEDNESDAY.

I am Grateful for -

Today I feel -

Daily thought.

THURSDAY.

I am Thankful for -

Today I would like to Attract -

Daily thought.

FRIDAY.

Today I am Grateful for -

I Wish -

Daily thought.

SATURDAY.

I am Thankful for -

Write or copy a Positive Affirmation -

Daily thought.

SUNDAY REVIEW.

What has been the best and worst part of your week?

Self-Refection / Self–Awareness.

MONDAY.

My Goal for this week is -

I am Thankful for -

Thought of the Day.

TUESDAY.

I am Grateful for -

I need -

Thought of the Day.

WEDNESDAY.

I am Thankful for -

Write down a quote that you like.

Daily thought.

THURSDAY.

I am Grateful for -

I Believe -

Random thought.

FRIDAY.

I am Thankful for -

Today I Pray for -

I Promise -

Pay yourself a compliment.

SATURDAY.

I am Grateful for -

____

____

____

I Can-

____

____

____

____

____

____

Daily thought.

____

____

____

____

____

____

____

____

____

SUNDAY REVIEW.

What has been the best and worst part of your week?

Self-Refection / Self–Awareness.

MONDAY.

My Goal for this week is -

I am Thankful for -

Thought of the Day.

TUESDAY.

I am Grateful for -

I Know -

Daily thought.

WEDNESDAY.

I am Thankful for -

I Attract -

I Will -

Write or copy a Positive Affirmation.

THURSDAY.

I am Grateful for -

___

___

___

Today I Pray for -

___

___

___

___

Thought of the Day.

___

___

___

___

___

___

___

___

___

___

FRIDAY.

I am Thankful for -

I AM -

Daily thought.

SATURDAY.

I am Grateful for -

I Promise -

Daily thought.

SUNDAY REVIEW.

What has been the best and worst part of your week?

Self-Refection / Self–Awareness.

MONDAY.

My Goal for this week is -

I am Thankful for -

Thought of the Day.

TUESDAY.

I am Thankful for -

I Love -

Thought of the Day.

WEDNESDAY.

I am Grateful for -

I Feel -

Today I Pray for -

Today I Attract -

THURSDAY.

I am Thankful for -

Today I let go of -

Thought of the Day.

FRIDAY.

I am Grateful for -

I Promise -

Write or copy a Positive Affirmation.

I love my Life because -

SATURDAY.

I am Thankful for -

I Forgive -

Daily Thought.

SUNDAY REVIEW.

What has been the best and worst part of your week?

Self-Refection / Self–Awareness.

MONDAY.

My Goal for this week is –

Today I am Grateful for –

Daily thought.

TUESDAY.

I am Thankful for -

Today I Pray for -

Daily thought.

WEDNESDAY.

I am Grateful for -

Today I feel -

Daily thought.

THURSDAY.

I am Thankful for -

Today I would like to Attract -

Daily thought.

FRIDAY.

Today I am Grateful for -

I Wish -

Daily thought.

SATURDAY.

I am Thankful for -

Write or copy a Positive Affirmation -

Daily thought.

SUNDAY REVIEW.

What has been the best and worst part of your week?

Self-Refection / Self–Awareness.

MONDAY.

My Goal for this week is -

I am Thankful for -

Thought of the Day.

TUESDAY.

I am Grateful for -

I need -

Thought of the Day.

WEDNESDAY.

I am Thankful for -

Write down a quote that you like.

Daily thought.

THURSDAY.

I am Grateful for -

I Believe -

Random thought.

FRIDAY.

I am Thankful for -

Today I Pray for -

I Promise -

Pay yourself a compliment.

SATURDAY.

I am Grateful for -

I Can-

Daily thought.

SUNDAY REVIEW.

What has been the best and worst part of your week?

Self-Refection / Self–Awareness.

MONDAY.

My Goal for this week is -

____

____

____

I am Thankful for -

____

____

____

Thought of the Day.

____

____

____

____

____

____

____

____

____

____

____

TUESDAY.

I am Grateful for -

I Know -

Daily thought.

WEDNESDAY.

I am Thankful for -

I Attract -

I Will -

Write or copy a Positive Affirmation.

THURSDAY.

I am Grateful for -

____

____

____

Today I Pray for -

____

____

____

____

Thought of the Day.

____

____

____

____

____

____

____

____

____

____

FRIDAY.

I am Thankful for -

I AM -

Daily thought.

SATURDAY.

I am Grateful for -

I Promise -

Daily thought.

SUNDAY REVIEW.

What has been the best and worst part of your week?

____

____

____

____

____

____

____

____

____

____

Self-Refection / Self–Awareness.

____

____

____

____

____

____

____

____

____

____

MONDAY.

My Goal for this week is -

I am Thankful for -

Thought of the Day.

TUESDAY.

I am Thankful for -

I Love -

Thought of the Day.

WEDNESDAY.

I am Grateful for -

I Feel -

Today I Pray for -

Today I Attract -

THURSDAY.

I am Thankful for -

Today I let go of -

Thought of the Day.

FRIDAY.

I am Grateful for -

I Promise -

Write or copy a Positive Affirmation.

I love my Life because -

SATURDAY.

I am Thankful for -

I Forgive -

Daily Thought.

SUNDAY REVIEW.

What has been the best and worst part of your week?

Self-Refection / Self–Awareness.

MONDAY.

My Goal for this week is –

Today I am Grateful for –

Daily thought.

TUESDAY.

I am Thankful for -

Today I Pray for -

Daily thought.

WEDNESDAY.

I am Grateful for -

Today I feel -

Daily thought.

THURSDAY.

I am Thankful for -

Today I would like to Attract -

Daily thought.

FRIDAY.

Today I am Grateful for -

I Wish -

Daily thought.

SATURDAY.

I am Thankful for -

Write or copy a Positive Affirmation -

Daily thought.

SUNDAY REVIEW.

What has been the best and worst part of your week?

Self-Refection / Self–Awareness.

MONDAY.

My Goal for this week is -

I am Thankful for -

Thought of the Day.

TUESDAY.

I am Grateful for -

I need -

Thought of the Day.

WEDNESDAY.

I am Thankful for -

Write down a quote that you like.

Daily thought.

THURSDAY.

I am Grateful for -

I Believe -

Random thought.

FRIDAY.

I am Thankful for -

Today I Pray for -

I Promise -

Pay yourself a compliment.

SATURDAY.

I am Grateful for -

I Can-

Daily thought.

SUNDAY REVIEW.

What has been the best and worst part of your week?

Self-Refection / Self–Awareness.

MONDAY.

My Goal for this week is -

I am Thankful for -

Thought of the Day.

TUESDAY.

I am Grateful for -

I Know -

Daily thought.

WEDNESDAY.

I am Thankful for -

I Attract -

I Will -

Write or copy a Positive Affirmation.

THURSDAY.

I am Grateful for -

Today I Pray for -

Thought of the Day.

FRIDAY.

I am Thankful for -

I AM -

Daily thought.

SATURDAY.

I am Grateful for -

I Promise -

Daily thought.

SUNDAY REVIEW.

What has been the best and worst part of your week?

Self-Refection / Self–Awareness.

MONDAY.

My Goal for this week is -

I am Thankful for -

Thought of the Day.

TUESDAY.

I am Thankful for -

I Love -

Thought of the Day.

WEDNESDAY.

I am Grateful for -

I Feel -

Today I Pray for -

Today I Attract -

THURSDAY.

I am Thankful for -

Today I let go of -

Thought of the Day.

FRIDAY.

I am Grateful for -

___

___

___

I Promise -

___

___

___

___

Write or copy a Positive Affirmation.

___

___

___

I love my Life because -

___

___

___

___

___

___

SATURDAY.

I am Thankful for -

I Forgive -

Daily Thought.

SUNDAY REVIEW.

What has been the best and worst part of your week?

Self-Refection / Self–Awareness.

MONDAY.

My Goal for this week is –

Today I am Grateful for –

Daily thought.

TUESDAY.

I am Thankful for -

Today I Pray for -

Daily thought.

WEDNESDAY.

I am Grateful for -

Today I feel -

Daily thought.

THURSDAY.

I am Thankful for -

Today I would like to Attract -

Daily thought.

FRIDAY.

Today I am Grateful for -

I Wish -

Daily thought.

SATURDAY.

I am Thankful for -

Write or copy a Positive Affirmation -

Daily thought.

SUNDAY REVIEW.

What has been the best and worst part of your week?

Self-Refection / Self–Awareness.

MONDAY.

My Goal for this week is -

I am Thankful for -

Thought of the Day.

TUESDAY.

I am Grateful for -

I need -

Thought of the Day.

WEDNESDAY.

I am Thankful for -

Write down a quote that you like.

Daily thought.

THURSDAY.

I am Grateful for -

I Believe -

Random thought.

FRIDAY.

I am Thankful for -

Today I Pray for -

I Promise -

Pay yourself a compliment.

SATURDAY.

I am Grateful for -

I Can-

Daily thought.

SUNDAY REVIEW.

What has been the best and worst part of your week?

Self-Refection / Self–Awareness.

MONDAY.

My Goal for this week is -

I am Thankful for -

Thought of the Day.

TUESDAY.

I am Grateful for -

____

____

____

I Know -

____

____

____

____

____

Daily thought.

____

____

____

____

____

____

____

____

____

____

WEDNESDAY.

I am Thankful for -

I Attract -

I Will -

Write or copy a Positive Affirmation.

THURSDAY.

I am Grateful for -

Today I Pray for -

Thought of the Day.

FRIDAY.

I am Thankful for -

___

___

___

I AM -

___

___

___

___

___

Daily thought.

___

___

___

___

___

___

___

___

___

___

SATURDAY.

I am Grateful for -

I Promise -

Daily thought.

SUNDAY REVIEW.

What has been the best and worst part of your week?

Self-Refection / Self–Awareness.

MONDAY.

My Goal for this week is -

I am Thankful for -

Thought of the Day.

TUESDAY.

I am Thankful for -

I Love -

Thought of the Day.

WEDNESDAY.

I am Grateful for -

I Feel -

Today I Pray for -

Today I Attract -

THURSDAY.

I am Thankful for -

Today I let go of -

Thought of the Day.

FRIDAY.

I am Grateful for -

I Promise -

Write or copy a Positive Affirmation.

I love my Life because -

SATURDAY.

I am Thankful for -

I Forgive -

Daily Thought.

SUNDAY REVIEW.

What has been the best and worst part of your week?

Self-Refection / Self–Awareness.

MONDAY.

My Goal for this week is –

Today I am Grateful for –

Daily thought.

TUESDAY.

I am Thankful for -

Today I Pray for -

Daily thought.

WEDNESDAY.

I am Grateful for -

Today I feel -

Daily thought.

THURSDAY.

I am Thankful for -

Today I would like to Attract -

Daily thought.

FRIDAY.

Today I am Grateful for -

I Wish -

Daily thought.

SATURDAY.

I am Thankful for -

Write or copy a Positive Affirmation -

Daily thought.

SUNDAY REVIEW.

What has been the best and worst part of your week?

Self-Refection / Self–Awareness.

MONDAY.

My Goal for this week is -

I am Thankful for -

Thought of the Day.

TUESDAY.

I am Grateful for -

I need -

Thought of the Day.

WEDNESDAY.

I am Thankful for -

Write down a quote that you like.

Daily thought.

THURSDAY.

I am Grateful for -

I Believe -

Random thought.

FRIDAY.

I am Thankful for -

Today I Pray for -

I Promise -

Pay yourself a compliment.

SATURDAY.

I am Grateful for -

I Can-

Daily thought.

SUNDAY REVIEW.

What has been the best and worst part of your week?

Self-Refection / Self–Awareness.

MONDAY.

My Goal for this week is -

I am Thankful for -

Thought of the Day.

TUESDAY.

I am Grateful for -

I Know -

Daily thought.

WEDNESDAY.

I am Thankful for -

I Attract -

I Will -

Write or copy a Positive Affirmation.

THURSDAY.

I am Grateful for -

Today I Pray for -

Thought of the Day.

FRIDAY.

I am Thankful for -

I AM -

Daily thought.

SATURDAY.

I am Grateful for -

I Promise -

Daily thought.

SUNDAY REVIEW.

What has been the best and worst part of your week?

Self-Refection / Self–Awareness.

MONDAY.

My Goal for this week is -

I am Thankful for -

Thought of the Day.

TUESDAY.

I am Thankful for -

I Love -

Thought of the Day.

WEDNESDAY.

I am Grateful for -

I Feel -

Today I Pray for -

Today I Attract -

THURSDAY.

I am Thankful for -

Today I let go of -

Thought of the Day.

FRIDAY.

I am Grateful for -

____

____

____

I Promise -

____

____

____

____

Write or copy a Positive Affirmation.

____

____

____

I love my Life because -

____

____

____

____

____

____

SATURDAY.

I am Thankful for -

I Forgive -

Daily Thought.

SUNDAY REVIEW.

What has been the best and worst part of your week?

Self-Refection / Self–Awareness.

MONDAY.

My Goal for this week is –

Today I am Grateful for –

Daily thought.

TUESDAY.

I am Thankful for -

Today I Pray for -

Daily thought.

WEDNESDAY.

I am Grateful for -

Today I feel -

Daily thought.

THURSDAY.

I am Thankful for -

Today I would like to Attract -

Daily thought.

FRIDAY.

Today I am Grateful for -

I Wish -

Daily thought.

SATURDAY.

I am Thankful for -

Write or copy a Positive Affirmation -

Daily thought.

SUNDAY REVIEW.

What has been the best and worst part of your week?

Self-Refection / Self–Awareness.

MONDAY.

My Goal for this week is -

I am Thankful for -

Thought of the Day.

TUESDAY.

I am Grateful for -

I need -

Thought of the Day.

WEDNESDAY.

I am Thankful for -

Write down a quote that you like.

Daily thought.

THURSDAY.

I am Grateful for -

I Believe -

Random thought.

FRIDAY.

I am Thankful for -

____

____

____

Today I Pray for -

____

____

____

____

I Promise -

____

____

____

____

Pay yourself a compliment.

____

____

____

____

____

SATURDAY.

I am Grateful for -

I Can-

Daily thought.

SUNDAY REVIEW.

What has been the best and worst part of your week?

Self-Refection / Self–Awareness.

MONDAY.

My Goal for this week is -

I am Thankful for -

Thought of the Day.

TUESDAY.

I am Grateful for -

I Know -

Daily thought.

WEDNESDAY.

I am Thankful for -

I Attract -

I Will -

Write or copy a Positive Affirmation.

THURSDAY.

I am Grateful for -

Today I Pray for -

Thought of the Day.

FRIDAY.

I am Thankful for -

I AM -

Daily thought.

SATURDAY.

I am Grateful for -

I Promise -

Daily thought.

SUNDAY REVIEW.

What has been the best and worst part of your week?

Self-Refection / Self–Awareness.

MONDAY.

My Goal for this week is -

I am Thankful for -

Thought of the Day.

TUESDAY.

I am Thankful for -

I Love -

Thought of the Day.

WEDNESDAY.

I am Grateful for -

I Feel -

Today I Pray for -

Today I Attract -

THURSDAY.

I am Thankful for -

Today I let go of -

Thought of the Day.

FRIDAY.

I am Grateful for -

I Promise -

Write or copy a Positive Affirmation.

I love my Life because -

SATURDAY.

I am Thankful for -

I Forgive -

Daily Thought.

SUNDAY REVIEW.

What has been the best and worst part of your week?

Self-Refection / Self–Awareness.

MONDAY.

My Goal for this week is –

Today I am Grateful for –

Daily thought.

TUESDAY.

I am Thankful for -

Today I Pray for -

Daily thought.

WEDNESDAY.

I am Grateful for -

Today I feel -

Daily thought.

THURSDAY.

I am Thankful for -

Today I would like to Attract -

Daily thought.

FRIDAY.

Today I am Grateful for -

I Wish -

Daily thought.

SATURDAY.

I am Thankful for -

Write or copy a Positive Affirmation -

Daily thought.

SUNDAY REVIEW.

What has been the best and worst part of your week?

Self-Refection / Self–Awareness.

MONDAY.

My Goal for this week is -

I am Thankful for -

Thought of the Day.

TUESDAY.

I am Grateful for -

I need -

Thought of the Day.

WEDNESDAY.

I am Thankful for -

Write down a quote that you like.

Daily thought.

THURSDAY.

I am Grateful for -

I Believe -

Random thought.

FRIDAY.

I am Thankful for -

Today I Pray for -

I Promise -

Pay yourself a compliment.

SATURDAY.

I am Grateful for -

I Can-

Daily thought.

SUNDAY REVIEW.

What has been the best and worst part of your week?

Self-Refection / Self–Awareness.

MONDAY.

My Goal for this week is -

I am Thankful for -

Thought of the Day.

TUESDAY.

I am Grateful for -

I Know -

Daily thought.

WEDNESDAY.

I am Thankful for -

I Attract -

I Will -

Write or copy a Positive Affirmation.

THURSDAY.

I am Grateful for -

Today I Pray for -

Thought of the Day.

FRIDAY.

I am Thankful for -

I AM -

Daily thought.

SATURDAY.

I am Grateful for -

I Promise -

Daily thought.

SUNDAY REVIEW.

What has been the best and worst part of your week?

Self-Refection / Self–Awareness.

MONDAY.

My Goal for this week is -

I am Thankful for -

Thought of the Day.

TUESDAY.

I am Thankful for -

I Love -

Thought of the Day.

WEDNESDAY.

I am Grateful for -

I Feel -

Today I Pray for -

Today I Attract -

THURSDAY.

I am Thankful for -

Today I let go of -

Thought of the Day.

FRIDAY.

I am Grateful for -

I Promise -

Write or copy a Positive Affirmation.

I love my Life because -

SATURDAY.

I am Thankful for -

I Forgive -

Daily Thought.

SUNDAY REVIEW.

What has been the best and worst part of your week?

Self-Refection / Self–Awareness.

MONDAY.

My Goal for this week is –

Today I am Grateful for –

Daily thought.

TUESDAY.

I am Thankful for -

Today I Pray for -

Daily thought.

WEDNESDAY.

I am Grateful for -

Today I feel -

Daily thought.

THURSDAY.

I am Thankful for -

Today I would like to Attract -

Daily thought.

FRIDAY.

Today I am Grateful for -

I Wish -

Daily thought.

SATURDAY.

I am Thankful for -

Write or copy a Positive Affirmation -

Daily thought.

SUNDAY REVIEW.

What has been the best and worst part of your week?

Self-Refection / Self–Awareness.

MONDAY.

My Goal for this week is -

I am Thankful for -

Thought of the Day.

TUESDAY.

I am Grateful for -

I need -

Thought of the Day.

WEDNESDAY.

I am Thankful for -

Write down a quote that you like.

Daily thought.

THURSDAY.

I am Grateful for -

I Believe -

Random thought.

FRIDAY.

I am Thankful for -

Today I Pray for -

I Promise -

Pay yourself a compliment.

SATURDAY.

I am Grateful for -

____

____

____

I Can-

____

____

____

____

____

____

Daily thought.

____

____

____

____

____

____

____

____

____

SUNDAY REVIEW.

What has been the best and worst part of your week?

Self-Refection / Self–Awareness.

MONDAY.

My Goal for this week is -

I am Thankful for -

Thought of the Day.

TUESDAY.

I am Grateful for -

I Know -

Daily thought.

WEDNESDAY.

I am Thankful for -

I Attract -

I Will -

Write or copy a Positive Affirmation.

THURSDAY.

I am Grateful for -

Today I Pray for -

Thought of the Day.

FRIDAY.

I am Thankful for -

I AM -

Daily thought.

SATURDAY.

I am Grateful for -

___

___

___

I Promise -

___

___

___

___

___

Daily thought.

___

___

___

___

___

___

___

___

___

___

SUNDAY REVIEW.

What has been the best and worst part of your week?

Self-Refection / Self–Awareness.

MONDAY.

My Goal for this week is -

I am Thankful for -

Thought of the Day.

TUESDAY.

I am Thankful for -

I Love -

Thought of the Day.

WEDNESDAY.

I am Grateful for -

I Feel -

Today I Pray for -

Today I Attract -

THURSDAY.

I am Thankful for -

Today I let go of -

Thought of the Day.

FRIDAY.

I am Grateful for -

I Promise -

Write or copy a Positive Affirmation.

I love my Life because -

SATURDAY.

I am Thankful for -

I Forgive -

Daily Thought.

SUNDAY REVIEW.

What has been the best and worst part of your week?

Self-Refection / Self–Awareness.

MONDAY.

My Goal for this week is –

Today I am Grateful for –

Daily thought.

TUESDAY.

I am Thankful for -

Today I Pray for -

Daily thought.

WEDNESDAY.

I am Grateful for -

Today I feel -

Daily thought.

THURSDAY.

I am Thankful for -

Today I would like to Attract -

Daily thought.

FRIDAY.

Today I am Grateful for -

I Wish -

Daily thought.

SATURDAY.

I am Thankful for -

Write or copy a Positive Affirmation -

Daily thought.

SUNDAY REVIEW.

What has been the best and worst part of your week?

Self-Refection / Self–Awareness.

MONDAY.

My Goal for this week is -

I am Thankful for -

Thought of the Day.

TUESDAY.

I am Grateful for -

I need -

Thought of the Day.

WEDNESDAY.

I am Thankful for -

Write down a quote that you like.

Daily thought.

THURSDAY.

I am Grateful for -

I Believe -

Random thought.

FRIDAY.

I am Thankful for -

Today I Pray for -

I Promise -

Pay yourself a compliment.

SATURDAY.

I am Grateful for -

I Can-

Daily thought.

SUNDAY REVIEW.

What has been the best and worst part of your week?

Self-Refection / Self–Awareness.

MONDAY.

My Goal for this week is -

I am Thankful for -

Thought of the Day.

TUESDAY.

I am Grateful for -

I Know -

Daily thought.

WEDNESDAY.

I am Thankful for -

I Attract -

I Will -

Write or copy a Positive Affirmation.

THURSDAY.

I am Grateful for -

Today I Pray for -

Thought of the Day.

FRIDAY.

I am Thankful for -

I AM -

Daily thought.

SATURDAY.

I am Grateful for -

____

____

____

I Promise -

____

____

____

____

____

Daily thought.

____

____

____

____

____

____

____

____

____

____

SUNDAY REVIEW.

What has been the best and worst part of your week?

Self-Refection / Self–Awareness.

MONDAY.

My Goal for this week is -

I am Thankful for -

Thought of the Day.

TUESDAY.

I am Thankful for -

I Love -

Thought of the Day.

WEDNESDAY.

I am Grateful for -

I Feel -

Today I Pray for -

Today I Attract -

THURSDAY.

I am Thankful for -

Today I let go of -

Thought of the Day.

FRIDAY.

I am Grateful for -

I Promise -

Write or copy a Positive Affirmation.

I love my Life because -

SATURDAY.

I am Thankful for -

I Forgive -

Daily Thought.

SUNDAY REVIEW.

What has been the best and worst part of your week?

Self-Refection / Self–Awareness.

MONDAY.

My Goal for this week is –

Today I am Grateful for –

Daily thought.

TUESDAY.

I am Thankful for -

Today I Pray for -

Daily thought.

WEDNESDAY.

I am Grateful for -

Today I feel -

Daily thought.

THURSDAY.

I am Thankful for -

Today I would like to Attract -

Daily thought.

FRIDAY.

Today I am Grateful for -

I Wish -

Daily thought.

SATURDAY.

I am Thankful for -

Write or copy a Positive Affirmation -

Daily thought.

SUNDAY REVIEW.

What has been the best and worst part of your week?

Self-Refection / Self–Awareness.

MONDAY.

My Goal for this week is -

I am Thankful for -

Thought of the Day.

TUESDAY.

I am Grateful for -

I need -

Thought of the Day.

WEDNESDAY.

I am Thankful for -

Write down a quote that you like.

Daily thought.

THURSDAY.

I am Grateful for -

I Believe -

Random thought.

FRIDAY.

I am Thankful for -

Today I Pray for -

I Promise -

Pay yourself a compliment.

SATURDAY.

I am Grateful for -

I Can-

Daily thought.

SUNDAY REVIEW.

What has been the best and worst part of your week?

Self-Refection / Self–Awareness.

MONDAY.

My Goal for this week is -

I am Thankful for -

Thought of the Day.

TUESDAY.

I am Grateful for -

I Know -

Daily thought.

WEDNESDAY.

I am Thankful for -

I Attract -

I Will -

Write or copy a Positive Affirmation.

THURSDAY.

I am Grateful for -

____

____

____

Today I Pray for -

____

____

____

____

Thought of the Day.

____

____

____

____

____

____

____

____

____

____

FRIDAY.

I am Thankful for -

I AM -

Daily thought.

SATURDAY.

I am Grateful for -

I Promise -

Daily thought.

SUNDAY REVIEW.

What has been the best and worst part of your week?

Self-Refection / Self–Awareness.

MONDAY.

My Goal for this week is -

I am Thankful for -

Thought of the Day.

TUESDAY.

I am Thankful for -

I Love -

Thought of the Day.

WEDNESDAY.

I am Grateful for -

I Feel -

Today I Pray for -

Today I Attract -

THURSDAY.

I am Thankful for -

____

____

____

Today I let go of -

____

____

____

____

____

____

Thought of the Day.

____

____

____

____

____

____

____

____

____

FRIDAY.

I am Grateful for -

I Promise -

Write or copy a Positive Affirmation.

I love my Life because -

SATURDAY.

I am Thankful for -

I Forgive -

Daily Thought.

SUNDAY REVIEW.

What has been the best and worst part of your week?

Self-Refection / Self–Awareness.

MONDAY.

My Goal for this week is –

____

____

____

Today I am Grateful for –

____

____

____

Daily thought.

____

____

____

____

____

____

____

____

____

____

____

TUESDAY.

I am Thankful for -

Today I Pray for -

Daily thought.

WEDNESDAY.

I am Grateful for -

Today I feel -

Daily thought.

THURSDAY.

I am Thankful for -

Today I would like to Attract -

Daily thought.

FRIDAY.

Today I am Grateful for -

I Wish -

Daily thought.

SATURDAY.

I am Thankful for -

Write or copy a Positive Affirmation -

Daily thought.

SUNDAY REVIEW.

What has been the best and worst part of your week?

Self-Refection / Self–Awareness.

MONDAY.

My Goal for this week is -

I am Thankful for -

Thought of the Day.

TUESDAY.

I am Grateful for -

I need -

Thought of the Day.

WEDNESDAY.

I am Thankful for -

Write down a quote that you like.

Daily thought.

THURSDAY.

I am Grateful for -

I Believe -

Random thought.

FRIDAY.

I am Thankful for -

Today I Pray for -

I Promise -

Pay yourself a compliment.

SATURDAY.

I am Grateful for -

I Can-

Daily thought.

SUNDAY REVIEW.

What has been the best and worst part of your week?

Self-Refection / Self–Awareness.

MONDAY.

My Goal for this week is -

I am Thankful for -

Thought of the Day.

TUESDAY.

I am Grateful for -

I Know -

Daily thought.

WEDNESDAY.

I am Thankful for -

I Attract -

I Will -

Write or copy a Positive Affirmation.

THURSDAY.

I am Grateful for -

Today I Pray for -

Thought of the Day.

FRIDAY.

I am Thankful for -

I AM -

Daily thought.

SATURDAY.

I am Grateful for -

I Promise -

Daily thought.

SUNDAY REVIEW.

What has been the best and worst part of your week?

Self-Refection / Self–Awareness.

MONDAY.

My Goal for this week is -

I am Thankful for -

Thought of the Day.

TUESDAY.

I am Thankful for -

I Love -

Thought of the Day.

WEDNESDAY.

I am Grateful for -

I Feel -

Today I Pray for -

Today I Attract -

THURSDAY.

I am Thankful for -

Today I let go of -

Thought of the Day.

FRIDAY.

I am Grateful for -

I Promise -

Write or copy a Positive Affirmation.

I love my Life because -

SATURDAY.

I am Thankful for -

I Forgive -

Daily Thought.

SUNDAY REVIEW.

What has been the best and worst part of your week?

Self-Refection / Self–Awareness.

Notes.

Notes.

Notes.

Made in the USA
Middletown, DE
20 April 2017